Gangs and Wanting to Belong

TOOKIE SPEAKS OUT AGAINST GANG VIOLENCE™

Stanley "Tookie" Williams

with Barbara Cottman Becnel

The Rosen Publishing Group's
PowerKids Press™
New York

Published in 1996 by The Rosen Publishing Group, Inc.
29 East 21st Street, New York, NY 10010

Copyright © 1996 by The Rosen Publishing Group, Inc.
Text copyright © by Barbara Cottman Becnel.

First Edition

Book design: Kim Sonsky

Photo credits: Cover © Bill Stanton/International Stock; front cover inset, back cover, and p. 4 © J. Patrick Forden; p. 7 by Lauren Piperno; p. 8 by Sarah Friedman; p. 11 by Kathleen McClancy; p. 12 © RIHA/Gamma Liaison; p. 15 © L. J. Schneider/International Stock; p. 16 © George Ancona/International Stock; p. 19 by Maria Moreno; p. 20 by Thomas Mangieri.

Williams, Stanley.
    Gangs and wanting to belong / Stanley "Tookie" Williams with Barbara Cottman Becnel.
        p.   cm. — (Tookie speaks out against gang violence)
    Includes index.
    Summary: A founder of the Crips discusses gangs, debunking the notion that belonging to a gang is the only way a kid can "fit in."
    ISBN 0-8239-2343-6
    1. Williams, Stanley—Juvenile literature. 2. Gang members—United States—Case studies—Juvenile literature. 3. Gangs—United States—Juvenile literature. 4. Group identity—United States—Juvenile literature. [1. Gangs. 2. Gang members. 3. Identity.] I. Becnel, Barbara Cottman. II. Title. III. Series: Williams, Stanley. Tookie speaks out against gang violence.
RC178.A1E25 1996
364.1'06'60973—dc20
                                                            96-1012
                                                            CIP
                                                            AC

Contents

Mama

My mother named me Stanley Williams after my father. But I only remember people calling me "Tookie," which is my nickname.

I'm from Shreveport, Louisiana. My father left us when I was a little boy. But my mother's sixteen sisters and brothers were always around. And so was my grandmother. We all called her Mama. I was Mama's favorite grandchild. I thought that as long as I had her, I had someone to **protect** (pro-TEKT) me. I had someone who made me feel special.

◀ *Even big, strong, tough guys need love and protection.*

Moving to South Central

I was about seven years old when my mother and I moved to South Central Los Angeles. I was sad. I thought I would never see my grandmother again. I thought I would never fit in anywhere else.

In South Central, I didn't know anyone. On my first **adventure** (ad-VEN-chur) outside alone, I got into a fight with a kid about my age. I learned that to fit in with the boys in South Central I would have to learn how to fight.

Some people think they need to hurt others to feel good about themselves. ▶

Growing Up, Fitting In

I became a good fighter because I wanted to fit in. By the time I reached high school, everyone knew how tough I was. In fact, a kid named Raymond Washington came up to me one day and said he and I should get together to fight our enemies. So we started a gang called the Crips.

Creating the Crips made it easy for us to fit in. We were the leaders. We decided what other kids had to do to fit in.

◀ *Some people join gangs to belong to a group.*

My Other Family

The number of guys in the Crips grew fast. The gang was like a second family for many of us. Some gang members felt closer to the Crips than to their real families. We even started calling each other "Cuz," for cousin.

Most Crips didn't have fathers living at home to teach them the right way to act or how to become men. So we learned from each other how to do bad things like steal cars, rob stores, and hurt people. We all thought that was what it took to be a man.

Gangs are not good places to learn how to be grown up. ▶

Gangs Aren't Good Families

Kids join gangs for all kinds of reasons. Many kids join to feel like they're a part of something, a family. But a gang is not a good family.

Raymond and I started the Crips to protect ourselves and our friends from other gangs. We wanted the protection of a family. But a good family leads its kids away from trouble. Our family, the Crips, led its kids right into trouble.

◄ *Gang members who break the law because their gang wants them to are often arrested.*

Everyone Wants to Fit In

Everyone wants to fit into a group. Your parents want to fit in at work. Your brothers and sisters want to fit in with their friends. You may want to fit in at school or Little League. These are all good things to fit in with. When you are a part of these things, you help yourself and you don't hurt others.

It's not good to fit in with people who hurt other people.

Everyone feels left out sometimes. ▶

Wanting to Belong

You may feel left out, like I did. You may not have anyone in your family to turn to. You may not have friends to talk things out with. Be **patient** (PAY-shent). Soon you'll meet kids who don't hurt others.

Gangs do bad things, such as steal cars, sell drugs, and hurt people. Do you want to do that? Do you want someone to hurt you? As much as you might want to fit in, don't join a gang. You won't find what you're looking for. All you will find is trouble, pain, and sadness. I know. I did.

◄ *It is better to feel left out than to belong to a group of people who hurt others.*

Making Good Choices

You may move to a new **neighborhood** (NAY-bur-hood) or go to a new school. You may be asked to join a violent gang or hang out with kids you don't like.

Remember that you always have a choice. It's up to you to **decide** (dee-SIDE) whom *you* want to be with and what group *you* want to belong to. Listen to yourself. If the kids you meet cause trouble, or hurt other people, or make you feel uncomfortable, it's better to be by yourself or to wait until you find other kids to spend time with.

It's your choice whom you spend time with. ▶

Standing Alone

Don't be afraid to stand alone. It's better than being with kids who hurt other people. You'll meet kids who don't hurt others. There were many times when I had to stand alone here in prison to stay away from violence.

I know how hard it is not to have friends. I also know how hard it is not to do something your friends want you to do. But I've learned not to care what other people, even my friends, think of me. I've learned to make my own good choices. I believe you can make the right choices too.

◀ *You can make smart choices about who your friends are and how you spend your time.*

Fitting in with Yourself

Most of my life I believed that I had to be bad to fit in. Most of the time I was acting. I didn't want to do bad things. I didn't want to hurt people. I did it to fit in. Now that I feel good about myself, I don't need to fit into any group that hurts people.

What you think about yourself is more important than what other kids think about you. Knowing what's right and what's wrong is more important than fitting in. Fit in with yourself. It is one of the best feelings in the world.

Glossary

adventure (ad-VEN-chur) Something exciting.
decide (dee-SIDE) To make a choice.
neighborhood (NAY-bur-hood) The area you live
    in.
patient (PAY-shent) Waiting calmly.
protect (pro-TEKT) To keep safe.

Index